Hot War–Cold War

Neil DeMarco

Hodder & Stoughton
A MEMBER OF THE HODDER HEADLINE GROUP

Acknowledgements

The front cover shows 'Gassed' :The Dressing Station at Le Bac-de-Sud, on the Doullens-ArrasRoady (detail), August 1918, by John Singer Sargent. Crown Copyright managed by Thr Imperial War Museum. Inset picture is reoroduced courtesy of Hulton Archive.

The publishers would like to thank the following individuals, institutions and companies for permission to reproduce copyright illustrations in this book:

Robert Hunt Library, page 19 top; Bettmann/Corbis, page 28 left and right; Bryn Colton/Assignments Photographers/Corbis, page 6; David Turnley/Corbis, page 25; Eason/Hulton © Steve Eason, page 24; Hulton-Deutsch Collection/Corbis, page 19 bottom; Hulton Getty, pages 2, 3, 7; Imperial War Museum, London, page 12 (Q6983); Marc Riboud/Magnum Photos, page 16; Neil DeMarco, pages 26 and 27; Rex Features, page 9.

The publishers would also like to thank the following for permission to reproduce material in this book:

Extracts from *The Collins Encyclopedia of Military History* by Ernest and Trevor Dupuy (HarperCollins, 1993), reproduced with permission of HarperCollins Publishers Ltd; Her Majesty's Stationery Office for an extract from *The Faber Book of Reportage*, edited by J. Carey; extracts from *The End of the American Century* by Jeffrey Robinson (Simon & Schuster, 1997) © Jeffrey Robinson, 1997; Copyright © Jeremy Isaacs Productions and Turner Original Productions 1998. Extracted from *The Cold War* by Jeremy Isaacs and Taylor Downing, published by Bantam Press, a division of Transworld Publishers. All rights reserved; Little Brown for the extract from *Nam* by Mark Baker (Abacus, 1982); an extract from *Why the Allies Won* by Richard Overy (Jonathan Cape, 1995). Used by permission of The Random House Group Limited; an extract from *Hiroshima Diary: The Journal of a Japanese Physician, August 6 – September 30, 1945* by Michihiko Hachiya, translated by Warner Wells, M.D. Copyright © 1955 by the University of North Carolina Press. Used with permission of the publisher.

Every effort has been made to trace and acknowledge ownership of copyright. The publishers will be glad to make suitable arrangements with any copyright holders whom it has not been possible to contact.

Orders: please contact Bookpoint Ltd, 130 Milton Park, Abingdon, Oxon OX14 4SB. Telephone: (44) 01235 827720, Fax: (44) 01235 400454. Lines are open from 9.00 – 6.00, Monday to Saturday, with a 24 hour message answering service.
Email address: orders@bookpoint.co.uk

British Library Cataloguing in Publication Data
A catalogue record for this title is available from The British Library

ISBN 0 340 79980 3

First published 2001
Impression number   10 9 8 7 6 5 4 3 2 1
Year   2005 2004 2003 2002 2001

Copyright © 2001 Neil DeMarco

All rights reserved. No part of this publication may be reproduced or transmitted in any form or by any means, electronic or mechanical, including photocopy, recording, or any information storage and retrieval system, without permission in writing from the publisher or under licence from the Copyright Licensing Agency Limited. Further details of such licences (for reprographic reproduction) may be obtained from the Copyright Licensing Agency Limited, of 90 Tottenham Court Road, London W1P 9HE.

Typeset by Liz Rowe
Printed in Great Britain for Hodder & Stoughton Educational, a division of Hodder Headline Plc, 338 Euston Road, London NW1 3BH by Printer Trento

WIRRAL SCHOOLS' LIBRARY SERVICE	
Supplier	Date 22.06.09
Acc no.	
Class 940.5	Group

Contents

1 How did the atomic bomb change the world? — 2
2 How did warfare change people's lives? — 4
3 How did wars affect the civilian population? — 6
4 How did the century's wars affect women? — 8
5 How did military technology change during the century? — 10
6 How did the role of the soldier change? — 12
7 How do wars start?
8 How do wars start?: nationalism and religion — 16
9 How did the Cold War start? — 18
10 Why was there a Cold War after the Second World War? — 20
11 Why did the Cold War not lead to a 'hot' war? — 22
12 How did the Cold War end? — 24
13 Local history and the Great War — 26
14 Why were so many people affected? — 28
Index — 30

1 HOW DID THE ATOMIC BOMB CHANGE THE WORLD?

CHECK OUT THE LINK
How did the Cold War start?

NEW WORDS

POLITICAL RELATIONS: the relations between the governments and leaders of different countries, as opposed, for example, to relations between sports teams.
RADIATION: the harmful effects of a nuclear explosion which include vomiting and diarrhoea; the most serious effect is leukaemia (cancer of the blood).

SOURCE A

◀ Hiroshima after the atomic explosion. Note how the heat of the blast has melted the steel ladder on the fire engine.

AKIRA'S TALE

The war had treated Hiroshima kindly. There had only been two air raids involving just a few aircraft on the city during the entire war.

Akira woke up early that Monday, 6 August 1945 and was happy to see that the sun was shining in a blue, cloudless sky. Suddenly the air-raid warning sounded at 7.09 a.m.

He quickly roused his mother and they made their way outside towards a shelter. They knew that their wooden house offered no protection against the fire-bombs the Americans often used. He could see four American B-29 bombers high in the sky. At 7.31 a.m. the all-clear was sounded. Akira breathed a sigh of relief and he began to think about what he would do that day. They returned to their home.

About 45 minutes later Akira went outside and noticed that there was still a plane in the sky. Why had they sounded the all-clear? At the same moment, Akira saw a blinding, pinkish white light about 500 metres above the ground and then the ground began to tremble. He saw a massive mushroom-shaped cloud rise up from the ground. What astonished him most was its beautiful pink colour. He felt a blast of hot air which lifted him off his feet and threw him across the street. The force of the blast knocked him unconscious. When he woke up he wondered why his burnt shirt was hanging down over his arms and then he realised it wasn't his shirt. It was his skin.

Akira decided that he must find his mother, though there was nothing left of his home. He began walking. Outside the offices of the Osaka Bank he saw a strange, remarkable sight. On the wall was a shadow of a sitting man; his elbow was on one knee and his chin was resting on his hand. That was all that was left of him. That was the moment of his death. Many others were also dead. Their charred corpses littered the streets and the burning buildings.

HOW DID THE ATOMIC BOMB CHANGE THE WORLD?

SOURCE B

The sight of the soldiers was more dreadful than the dead people in the river. Where their skin had peeled, their flesh was wet and mushy. Their eyes, noses and ears had been burned away, and it looked like their ears had melted off.

I saw reservoirs filled to the brim with people who looked as though they had been boiled alive.

▲ Quoted in Hiroshima Diary by Michihiko Hachiya (1955).

SOURCE C

▲ Tokyo after the fire-raid of March 1945.

One woman was still alive, her leg trapped under a heavy beam in the ruins of a building. It was too heavy to move. A man was cutting off her leg with a rusty saw to get her free. People were walking, stumbling about, their skin hanging about them in shreds. Blood oozed from their eyes and from holes where their eyes had been. Akira noticed one woman pleading for help. The flesh from her side had been burned away and he could see her ribs.

THE DESTROYER OF WORLDS

The bomb which exploded above Hiroshima that day was the first atomic bomb used in war. It was not remarkable just because 70,000 people died that day. The Americans had killed 85,000 Japanese civilians in one fire-bomb raid on Tokyo in March 1945, but that raid had involved *300* B-29 bombers. Now an entire city had been destroyed by a single bomb dropped by just one plane.

But it wasn't just the devastating power of the explosion that made this bomb different. The long-term effects of this bomb would go on killing for years afterwards. The effects of the **radiation** from the explosion went on to kill another 130,000 people by 1951.

The bombs were developed in the 1950s and were 250 times more powerful than those previously used. Mankind now had the power to destroy the world in a nuclear war. This is why the weapon was so terrible.

THE SOVIET UNION'S FEARS

Political relations between the USA and the world's first Communist country, the Soviet Union (what is now mostly Russia) began to worsen in 1945. The Russians didn't yet have the technology to develop their own nuclear weapon and were afraid that the USA might use theirs against them. This tension and hostility between the world's two great powers was later called the Cold War. It lasted until the early 1990s.

Q Think about it …

1. Describe in a paragraph the immediate and long-term effects of the atomic bomb on the people of Hiroshima.

2. Using the sources and text, make out an argument that:

■ the bombing of Hiroshima was not any more terrible than the fire-bombing of Tokyo in March 1945;

■ the bombing of Hiroshima was much more terrible than the raid on Tokyo.

3. Why could the Hiroshima bombing be described as the start of a whole new chapter in the the history of warfare?

2 HOW DID WARFARE CHANGE PEOPLE'S LIVES?

This chapter sets out to answer one big question: why did the conflicts of the twentieth century affect so many people? The answer to a question like this is made up of several other questions which connect to this big question, and some of these questions are also linked to each other. In a way, the whole investigation is a bit like a giant spider's web, simlar to that shown in **Source C**.

This investigation is about conflict, but it's not just about wars. A major part of this book is about the cold war between the USA and the Soviet Union. These two countries never actually fought each other directly in the twentieth century, but after 1945 they often faced each other angrily in a *political* war. **Source C** shows you the ways in which the Cold War developed as well as the reasons for real or 'hot' wars taking place.

SOURCE A

▲ A First World War British Sopwith Camel. The war began with planes like this. It had a maximum speed of 188km/h (117mph). It carried two machine guns and four 11kg bombs.

WERE THE CONFLICTS OF THE LAST CENTURY DIFFERENT FROM PREVIOUS ONES?

There is nothing new about mankind fighting wars, and you might think that the wars of the last century weren't much different from wars in earlier centuries. But the conflicts of the twentieth century were very different in important ways. This investigation sets out to show how twentieth-century warfare was vastly different from previous wars – both for soldiers and civilians. Women, for example, played a very important role in keeping up factory production in both world wars, especially in Britain.

However, perhaps the *causes* of conflict in the last century were much the same. Religion and rivalry between nations over territory were common causes of war in the past, and they played a part in the twentieth century's wars too. So, the twentieth century and its history is not always about change. Sometimes it's about continuity, or how things stay the same and don't change.

Chapter 1 touched on a very important difference between the twentieth century and previous centuries. The development of nuclear weapons, such as the atomic bomb dropped on Hiroshima, meant that from the 1950s onwards man had the power to destroy the planet. This had never been possible before. It meant that every confrontation in the Cold War between the USA and the Soviet Union could have led to a final, catastrophic nuclear war which would have cost the lives of hundreds of millions of people. The Cuban Missile Crisis in 1962 (see Chapter 11) is an example of such a confrontation.

HOW DID WARFARE CHANGE PEOPLE'S LIVES?

SOURCE B

1980s Tornado. This British- Italian- and German-designed fighter-bomber flies at a maximum speed of 1,482km/h (921mph). It carries a bomb load of 9,070kgs, and has missiles, guided by laser, which can hit a target 50kms (30 miles) away. It can also carry nuclear weapons. ▼

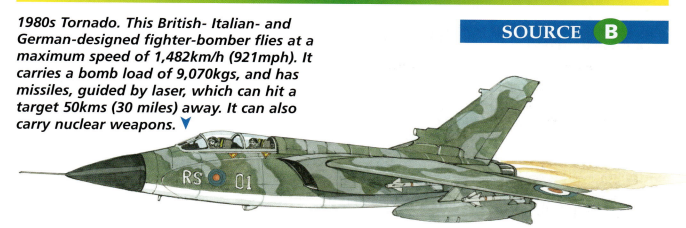

SOURCE C

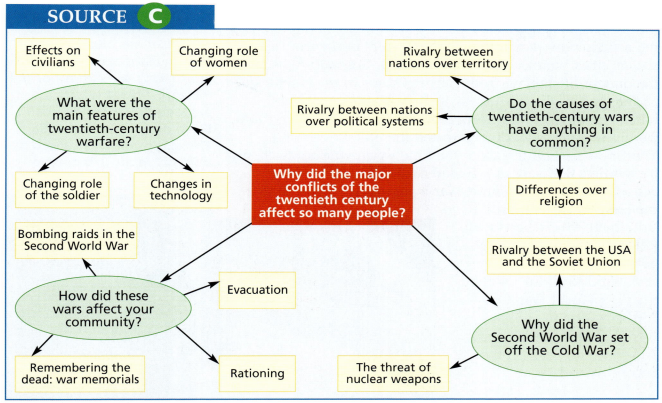

▲ History web

Q Think about it …

1. Compare the two aircraft in **Sources A** and **B**. How much has military technology changed in the 70 years between these two planes?

2. Using the history web diagram as your source, write four paragraphs under each of the four main headings, i.e.:

   a. What were the main features of twentieth-century warfare?

   b. Do the causes of twentieth-century wars have anything in common?

   c. Why did the Second World War set off the Cold War?

   d. How did these wars affect your community?

You can base your paragraphs around the additional points coming off the main headings.

3 HOW DID WARS AFFECT THE CIVILIAN POPULATION?

CHECK OUT THE LINK
How did the century's wars affect women?

NEW WORDS
ATROCITY: an extremely cruel act.
GENOCIDE: the deliberate killing of a very large number of people from a particular race, nation or religion.

CIVILIANS IN THE FRONT LINE

When the First World War started in 1914 the main worry of civilians was that their loved ones would have to fight. Fathers, sons and brothers now risked losing their lives or being wounded – but that was how it had always been. However, this war would bring a terrible new experience for the civilian population: enemy action. The aeroplane and the airship now meant that civilians were in the front line too, as cities were occasionally bombed. Coastal towns faced the danger of shelling from German ships in the North Sea.

The scale of the air raids over British cities was small when compared to the Second World War. But it meant that from now on wars would threaten the life of everyone. There was no going back to the time when warfare was only for soldiers and sailors. Civilian casualties from enemy action in the Second World War were much greater than in the First World War. In Britain 60,000 civilians were killed by enemy air raids between 1940 and 1945 compared to about 1,400 in the First World War. Over 750,000 German civilians were killed in British and American air raids in the Second World War.

THE 'FORGOTTEN HOLOCAUSTS'

It's worth pointing out that both sides deliberately bombed the civilian population in the Second World War. They weren't killed accidentally as the bombers searched for industrial targets like factories. Both the Japanese and Germans wanted to dominate their parts of the world. But they also believed that they had a right to do this because they were racially superior to their neighbours. The Japanese carried out terrible **atrocities** against the 'inferior' Chinese in Nanjing (Nanking) in 1937 and 1938. Perhaps as many as 200,000 civilians were murdered, mutilated and raped by the Japanese in a six-week period.

Terrorism has also meant that civilians are in the front line. This is the cockpit of the Pan-Am 747 jet which exploded over the Scottish town of Lockerbie in 1988. The explosion was caused by a bomb. In all, 270 people died. ▼

SOURCE A

HOW DID WARS AFFECT THE CIVILIAN POPULATION?

SOURCE B

▲ French civilians in 1945 searching rubbish bins for scraps of food. Most civilian populations face hunger during war, but several million people may have starved to death during the Second World War.

The Nazis deliberately set out to murder an entire civilian population: Europe's 11 million Jews. They managed 6 million before Germany's defeat in 1945 ended their murderous campaign. No doubt you know something of that Holocaust already. But what do you know about the Armenian **genocide** of 1915–16 in which 1.5 million Christian Armenian civilians died at the hands of the Muslim Turks? Religion as well as race played a part in this. Did you know that in 1971, troops from West Pakistan massacred between 1 and 3 million Bengali civilians in East Pakistan (now Bangladesh)? Here the reason wasn't religious or racial but political. East Pakistan wanted to break away from West Pakistan and rule itself.

As the century ended nothing had changed. In what used to be called Yugoslavia, during 1992–95, Christian Serbs attacked the Muslim population of Bosnia, killing and raping them and burning their homes as they tried to 'cleanse' the area of Muslims. The list of civilian populations murdered for religious, racial or political reasons in the twentieth century is, sadly, a long one. There is little reason to think that the twenty-first century will be much different.

Q Think about it ...

Civilians have died in the twentieth century's wars for many different reasons. These conflicts have been caused by:

- power struggles between countries, such as the First and Second World Wars;
- racial hatred between different races;
- religious hatred between peoples of different religions;
- terrorism caused by terrorist groups killing civilians to achieve their aims.

Write a paragraph under each of the four categories above, describing the different ways civilians have been affected by conflicts involving these reasons. For example, you could mention how between 1 and 3 million Bengali civilians were killed by West Pakistan as part of a power struggle between West and East Pakistan in 1971. You should use the information in this chapter and any of your own knowledge of other conflicts. For example, many civilians have been killed in Northern Ireland. Into which categories would you put their deaths?

4 HOW DID THE CENTURY'S WARS AFFECT WOMEN?

> **CHECK OUT THE LINK**
> How did wars affect the civilian population?

NEW WORDS
ARMED FORCES: army, navy and air force.
COMBATANT: someone involved in actual fighting.
EVACUATION: the removal of civilians – especially children – from areas likely to be affected by enemy action.
MUNITIONS: the weapons of war, such as shells, guns and bullets.
RATIONING: limiting the amount of essential supplies, especially food, which people can buy.

Women have always been the victims of war, experiencing murder, rape, the loss of their loved ones, and the destruction of their homes. The twentieth century was no different. These things still happened. Indeed, rape was used as a weapon in the civil war in the former Yugoslavia in the 1990s in order to terrorise populations to leave certain areas. However, there is a difference in the way wars in the last century affected women. For the first time, women played a key role in the wars themselves – not as victims but as participants in helping to win these wars.

SOURCE A

I remember one boy came in whose arms and legs had all been amputated and both eyes were injured. He said, 'I know I don't have any arms, and I know I don't have any legs, but just tell my mother I love her.' I began crying, right there. I don't know if he lived or died, I don't want to know. You couldn't know. That is why I tried never to learn their last names.

◀ *An American nurse in the Vietnam War in the late 1960s remembers one wounded soldier. Quoted in* Women in War *by Shelley Saywell (1985).*

WOMEN IN THE FACTORIES

The First World War would be won by the side which could keep producing enough coal, steel and iron to make the weapons the soldiers needed. Gradually, all the countries involved in the war realised that they had to replace these workers with women.

By the end of the war there were 900,000 women working in the **munitions** industry, up from 200,000 in 1914. Women also worked in shipyards and drove trams, buses and ambulances.

During the Second World War mothers with young children were evacuated from the major cities, industrial areas and ports which the enemy were likely to bomb. **Evacuation** wasn't popular. The host families which received the evacuees weren't given any choice and often they weren't very welcoming. Arrangements had to be made between the families as to what times they would use the kitchen, for example. Some of the evacuated families came from poor, inner-city areas and their behaviour shocked their hosts in the countryside.

Rationing was another major problem faced by women. Many women worked long shifts in their factories – sometimes 12 hours at a time. After work they faced long queues for rationed goods and then, when they finally got home, they had to cook the family meal. Marriages often couldn't stand the strain which the war created. In 1939 only 1 British marriage in every 100 ended in divorce. By 1945 it had gone up to 5 in every 100.

Wars change people. The Second World War changed many women. At the end of the war women were more confident of their abilities and more determined to get the equal

HOW DID THE CENTURY'S WARS AFFECT WOMEN?

rights to which they now felt they were entitled – though it would be 20 years before real progress was made. Wars in the twentieth century also showed that women are not always just the victims of violence. Sometimes they can be its cause (see **Source C**).

WOMEN IN UNIFORM

Nearly half-a-million British women served in the armed forces in the Second World War, but the nearest they got to combat was operating anti-aircraft guns. Churchill, the prime minister at the time, insisted that only men could actually fire the gun. Working on anti-aircraft guns was dangerous, and many of the 335 British women killed in army uniform during the war were gun crews. (The Soviet Union was the only country to use women in combat. Russian women proved especially effective as fighter pilots and snipers.) Women in the **armed forces** normally did less dangerous jobs, but this meant that the men who usually did them could now be sent to fight.

The usual role for women in uniform during this and all wars in the century was as nurses. In one sense it is a typically female role: caring for sick and wounded men. The traditional image of the young nurse in her starched, clean, white uniform is the one governments have always wanted to show. The reality – whatever the war – was always different (see **Source A**).

WOMEN AT HOME

Many more women, though, have had to live through wars as mothers, trying to raise and care for their families while dealing with the daily threat of death. In the Second World War, as we have seen, civilian women were part of the front line because aircraft could bomb their homes (see **Source B**) or enemy troops occupy their towns.

SOURCE B

To my left I suddenly see a woman. I can see her to this day and shall never forget it. She carries a bundle in her arms. It is a baby. She runs, she falls, and the child flies in an arc into the fire … The woman remains lying on the ground completely still … I stumbled on towards where it was dark. Suddenly, I saw people again, right in front of me. They scream and wave with their hands, and then – to my utter horror and amazement – I see how one after another they simply seem to let themselves drop to the ground. I had a feeling that they were being shot. Today I know that these unfortunate people were the victims of lack of oxygen.

SOURCE C

▲ This is a photograph of a 16-year-old Syrian girl. It was taken in 1985 just before she drove a car packed with explosives into an Israeli patrol in Lebanon. She blew herself to pieces and killed two Israeli soldiers.

Q *Think about it …*

The conflicts of the twentieth century have affected women in many different ways. Describe in a series of paragraphs (which you can also illustrate) how women have played important roles in:

a. industry during the First and Second World Wars;
b. the armed forces, in some cases as **combatants**;
c. nursing;
d. maintaining family life.

◀ Margaret Freyer, a German woman, describes the fire-bombing of Dresden by British and American bombers in 1945. Quoted in *The Faber Book of Reportage*, edited by J. Carey, (1987).

5 HOW DID MILITARY TECHNOLOGY CHANGE DURING THE CENTURY?

CHECK OUT THE LINK
How do you think the changes in military technology discussed in this chapter affected the civilian population?

THE TECHNOLOGY OF KILLING

In 1914 machine-guns were new weapons of war. They could fire around eight or nine bullets a second compared to just one every three or four seconds for a soldier with a rifle. Medium-sized artillery guns could fire a shell weighing 7kg a distance of 8km. The shell could be made to explode in the air, showering the soldiers beneath it with hundreds of lethal, marble-sized steel balls (see **Source A**). One French gun was so big it could only move on railway tracks. It fired a 900kg shell a distance of 16km.

In 1914 artillery gunners had to guess the distance of the target, and the only way they could tell if the shell hit the target was by placing a 'spotter' in a good position with a pair of binoculars or by relying on aircraft to see how accurate the shot was. Either way, the gunners then had to use signals or have messages dropped to them from the plane (see **Source B**).

No doubt troops in 1914 thought that weapons' technology couldn't go much further. But, of course, they were very wrong. Today, machine-guns mounted on aircraft can fire over a 160 bullets a second. While artillery is still important, armies have developed guided missiles which can be fired from ships or aircraft. The location of the target is put into the missile's computer, and it then works out the best route to the target. It avoids buildings and follows the outline of the terrain until it hits the target (see **Source C**). The cruise missile can travel 2,500km at a speed of 660kph. The makers of this missile claim that it could be made to pass between the goal posts on a football field at a distance of several hundred kilometres.

▲ **SOURCE A** The effect of shrapnel from an exploding shell falling on soldiers.

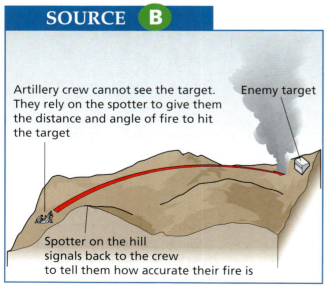

▲ **SOURCE B** Hitting a hidden target during the First World War with artillery.

HOW DID MILITARY TECHNOLOGY CHANGE DURING THE CENTURY?

SOURCE C

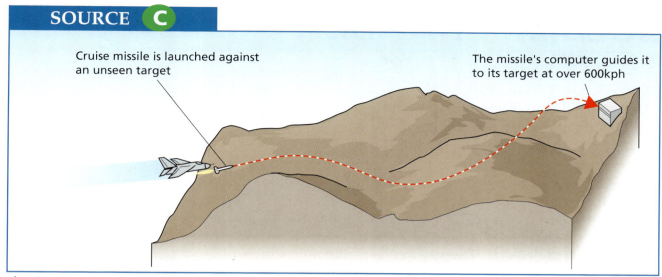

▲ Hitting a hidden target in 1990 with a cruise missile fired from an aircraft.

SMARTER THAN THE AVERAGE BOMB?

Weapons like cruise or Tomahawk missiles were used with some degree of success in the 1991 Gulf War against Iraq, but they weren't as accurate as the Americans claimed at the time. Only half the 288 Tomahawk missiles fired during the war hit their target and not the 240 or so the American forces claimed at the time. There were also doubts about the accuracy of British and American bombing in the campaign in Kosovo in 1999. Nonetheless, these so-called 'smart' weapons did achieve some remarkable strikes. The pilot could follow the path of the bomb or missile on a television screen and direct it onto the target using a laser beam.

MEGATON MADNESS

These weapons, despite their dazzling technology, are not particularly destructive when compared to nuclear weapons. During the last 50 years of the twentieth century the destructive power of nuclear weapons increased remarkably. The bomb dropped on Hiroshima in 1945 had 15kt (kilotons) of explosive power. That is the same as 15,000 tons of TNT (trinitrotoluene) explosive.

It has been estimated that in 1980 the USA and the Soviet Union had between them a nuclear capacity of 14,000mt of TNT: enough to cause nearly 1 million 'Hiroshimas'.

Clearly, the human race was now quite capable of destroying itself. Fortunately, as we shall see in later chapters, the Russians and the Americans realised just how dangerous and ridiculous the situation had become. Towards the end of the 1980s serious negotiations began between the two great powers with a view to reducing their stocks of nuclear weapons.

Think about it ...

1. Compare **Sources B** and **C**. Explain in a few sentences how far technology improved between the First World War and the Gulf War in 1990.

2. Warfare had become very 'high-tech' by the end of the twentieth century. Can you think of any disadvantages, from a military point of view, of using advanced electronics, computers and lasers to make these weapons work?

3. Can you suggest any reasons to explain how the Americans and the Russians had got to the situation where they had the power to destroy the planet with a million Hiroshimas? (Clues: think about the Cold War; fear and uncertainty about the enemy's power.)

6 HOW DID THE ROLE OF THE SOLDIER CHANGE?

CHECK OUT THE LINK
Do you think soldiers involved in the 'high tech' wars of the late twentieth century would find wars less terrifying than those at the start of the century?

NEW WORDS
CONSCRIPT: a man called up to fight by the government and who has no choice.
PATRIOTISM: love of your country.
PROFESSIONALS: people who choose the armed forces as a career.

The technology of warfare certainly changed a great deal during the twentieth century, as you will have read in the last chapter. What is less clear is whether what it was like to fight in a war changed. Did a soldier going 'over the top' in an infantry charge feel differently to one facing an enemy in Vietnam or the Falklands? Did they feel differently about killing another human being or do people feel the same things in war, no matter how far apart they are in time?

WHY DID SOLDIERS FIGHT?
Men went to war in 1914 for many different reasons. Some clearly wanted to fight because of **patriotism** and felt their country had to be defended against an aggressive enemy. Some fought because of peer-group pressure – because their mates were joining up and they didn't want to be left out. This applied more to Britons than other nationalities because Britain depended on volunteers until 1916. For some men, war was a glorious, romantic adventure.

Generally, most men in the trenches in the First World War soon lost the early enthusiasm which came with these reasons. They soon realised that war was not an adventure. Neither could patriotism have been enough to keep men going through the terrible conditions and dangers of that war. Many soldiers later talked of how one feeling above all others kept them going: comradeship. Comradeship is the closeness, affection and loyalty which men feel for one other when they face the same extreme dangers together. They carried on fighting because they didn't want to let their mates down.

Patriotism was important for soldiers in other wars too. The men who fought in the Second World War felt just as patriotic as those in the First, but they went to war

SOURCE A

▲ A British soldier gives a drink to a wounded German prisoner in August 1918. Generally, wounded prisoners were well treated by both sides.

without the enthusiasm of the men in 1914. By 1939 men had a much better idea of what warfare in the twentieth century was really like. An important factor in this was that the men who fought in the Second World War were **conscripts** – they had to fight. This is also true for the Americans who fought in the Vietnam War (1965–73). But the Britons who fought in the Falklands (1982) against Argentina were **professionals** and there was much more enthusiasm for that war. It was what they had trained for.

12

HOW DID THE ROLE OF THE SOLDIER CHANGE?

SOURCE B

I sobbed: 'I'm sorry.' Then I threw up all over myself. I recognised the half-digested ration beans dribbling down my front and smelled the vomit. At the same time I noticed another odour; I had urinated in my trousers.

▲ *William Manchester describing his experience of killing a Japanese soldier for the first time. Quoted in* Goodbye Darkness, *by William Manchester (1982).*

SOURCE C

We used to cut their ears off. If a guy had a necklace of ears, he was a good killer. It was encouraged to cut ears off, to cut the nose off, to cut the guy's penis off. A female, you cut her breasts off. It was encouraged to do these things. The officers expected you to do it or something was wrong with you.

▲ *A US soldier on his time in Vietnam. Quoted in* Nam *by Mark Baker (1982).*

SOURCE D

As I rolled him over to identify him, he had actually had a shot that had just gone through the side of his left eye and taken away the side of his left skull. He was a soldier who I knew had got a young family. And I suddenly realised that our strength lay in the fact that we all knew each other, and would do what was needed because we were friends. Not because the Queen wanted us to do it, or Mrs. Thatcher… but… because we were friends.

▲ *David Cooper, a British chaplain in the Falklands War, describes a dead British soldier. Quoted in* The Falklands War *by Denys Blakeway (1992).*

 Think about it …

War caused men to experience many different emotions. Some of these are shown in the five sources in this chapter.

1. Complete the chart below, showing which sources show which emotions and why. An example has been done for you.
2. Do you think that soldiers who kill prisoners or do things like those in **Source C** should be punished?
3. Using all these sources explain in about 100 words how war can affect soldiers taking part in it.

Emotion	Found in source/s	Supporting evidence from the source
Hatred of the enemy		
Comradeship		
Cruelty		
Guilt		
Kindness		
Fear	Source B	'I had urinated in my trousers' shows that the soldier had been very frightened at the time.

7 HOW DO WARS START?

CHECK OUT THE LINK
How did nationalism and religion cause conflict?
Why was there a Cold War after the Second World War?

NEW WORDS

ALLIES: two or more countries linked to each other in an alliance to give support if a war breaks out.

SOURCE A

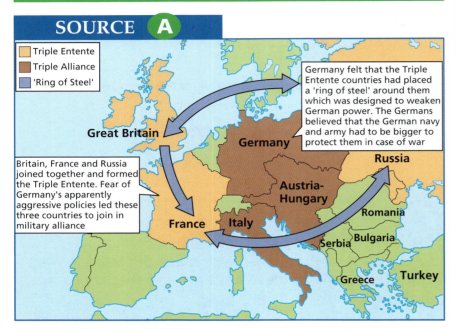

◀ Map of the alliance systems in 1914.

THE FIRST WORLD WAR

The causes of major events like wars are never simple. Historians, for example, argue endlessly over the causes of the First World War (1914–18). One approach is to divide causes into types. For example, the First World War had long- and short-term causes. The long-term causes helped to bring about the war *eventually* but they didn't decide when that war would happen. Short-term causes, on the other hand, decided *when* the war would break out.

GREAT POWER RIVALRY

The war broke out in 1914 after a long period of tension between Europe's Great Powers. On the one side was Britain, France and Russia (called the Entente Powers) and on the other was Germany and Austria (called the Central Powers). Each side feared the other and was convinced that it had aggressive plans.

MURDER IN SARAJEVO

So, there were many long-term causes which were adding to the tension in Europe but these had been going on for more than ten years without a war happening. What was missing was the short-term cause which would set the whole thing off. This spark finally ignited in June 1914. In that month, the heir to the throne of the Austrian empire was assassinated by a group of Bosnian Serbs living in Austria. They wanted Bosnia to be part of Serbia. The Austrians blamed the government of Serbia and used this as an excuse to declare war on Serbia on July 28 1914.

The conflict might not have spread any further but for the fact that Serbia was supported by Russia, and so Russia threatened Austria. From here the alliance system kicked in as the powers rushed in to support their allies. By August 4, the two alliance systems were at war with each other.

THE SECOND WORLD WAR

The causes of the Second World War (1939–45) were also long- and short-term. The Treaty of Versailles (1919) which ended the First World War was itself a cause of the Second World War. The Germans thought the terms were harsh and unfair and Hitler used this anger to help him to get to power in 1933.

As soon as he was in power, Hitler began expanding Germany's armed forces (rearmament). Once again Britain and France began to fear Germany's military power – just as they had in the years before 1914. Britain and France tried to negotiate

HOW DO WARS START?

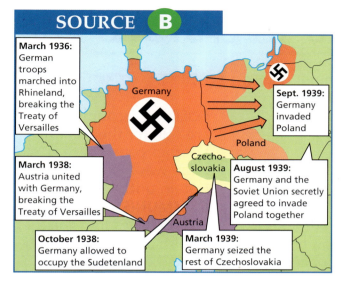

◀ Map of Europe in the 1930s.

with Hitler and agree to some of his demands. This policy of agreeing to Hitler's demands in order to avoid war is called 'appeasement'. Britain's prime minister from 1937, Neville Chamberlain, believed that a war with a powerful Germany would be a disaster for an unprepared Britain.

MUNICH

The British and French accepted Germany's rearmament policy and take-over of Austria in 1938 – despite the fact that these were both against the terms of the Treaty of Versailles. The events of March 1938, October 1939, and then March 1939 (see **Source B**) convinced Hitler that Britain and France would never stand up to him. Chamberlain and the French at last realised that Hitler could not be trusted to keep his word. They both promised the Poles that they would declare war on Germany if Hitler invaded Poland.

THE NAZI-SOVIET PACT

On August 24, 1939 the Germans signed a treaty with the Soviet Union not to go to war with each other. Secretly, they agreed to invade Poland and share it between them. Hitler was now ready to seize Poland. Just a week later, on September 1, 1939, Germany invaded Poland as planned. To Hitler's surprise and annoyance both Britain and France stood by their promise to the Poles and declared war on Germany two days later.

Q Think about it ...

This exercise is about dividing up the causes of the two world wars into long- and short-term and then seeing what the similarities and differences are.

1. Title your page 'Causes of the First World War'. Divide your page into two columns. Head each column 'Long-term' and 'Short-term'. Put into the correct column each of the following causes:

- the rival alliance systems of the Great Powers encouraged both sides to behave more aggressively;
- the heir to the throne of the Austrian Empire was assassinated by Serbian Nationalists in June 1914;
- both sides had been building up their military power, especially their navies;
- each side felt threatened by the other.

2. Now do the same for the causes of the Second World War, putting into the correct column each of the following causes:

- Germany's resentment against the Treaty of Versailles;
- the British and French policy of appeasement towards Hitler;
- Germany's rearmament policy increasing German military power;
- Britain and France's promise to defend Poland;
- The Nazi–Soviet pact.

3. 'The First and Second World Wars both have one cause in common: both sides were afraid of the other side's military power.' Explain whether you agree or disagree with this interpretation.

8 HOW DO WARS START?: NATIONALISM AND RELIGION

Conflicts can start for different reasons. One common cause of conflict in the half century after 1945 was religion. Of course, wars or conflicts are rarely caused by just one reason. Quite often several reasons link together – **nationalism** and religion, for example.

NATIONALISM AFTER 1945: VIETNAM

One of the consequences of the Second World War was an increase in the desire of many peoples living in **colonies** to become **independent**. Many of these colonies had helped the ruling power defeat the Germans and the Japanese. India, for example, had provided over 2.5 million troops to help Britain, the largest army of volunteers in history. After the war, most Indians felt they had done enough to earn the right to rule themselves. The British government agreed and India became independent in 1947.

Not all European powers took this attitude. France, for example, refused to allow Vietnam to become independent. The result was a war between the **Communist** North Vietnamese, led by Ho Chi Minh, and the French. It lasted from 1946 to 1954 and ended with the French pulling out of Vietnam. People were surprised that a badly equipped, mostly peasant army could defeat a highly trained and modern European army. What mattered here was not the level of equipment but the willingness to fight. The Vietnamese fought to free their country from French rule and this made all the difference.

This great belief in their cause is a common feature of nationalist fighters in the decades after 1945. Once the North Vietnamese had beaten the French they faced the USA. The Americans strongly opposed Communism and wanted to stop it spreading so they supported the anti-Communist government of South Vietnam. The war against the USA was tough but it also ended in victory. The Americans pulled out of South Vietnam in 1973 and two years later the North Vietnamese army reunited the whole of the country. Once again, the power of nationalism had proved itself able to win against the odds.

NEW WORDS

COLONY: a country or area under the rule of another country – e.g. India was a colony of Britain until 1947.

COMMUNIST: someone who believes that the wealth of a country, such as land and factories, should be controlled by the state and that there should only be one political party.

GUERRILLA FIGHTERS: fighters using hit-and-run raids and ambushes but avoiding major battles.

INDEPENDENT: a country becomes independent when it begins to rule itself with its own government.

NATIONALISM: the desire to free your country from foreign control or to have your country dominate others.

SOURCE A

> The Americans believed that they could bomb North Vietnam into defeat by cutting off supplies to its troops. But the Vietnamese, as you can see in this photograph, used whatever methods they could to keep their troops supplied with food and weapons.

SOURCE B

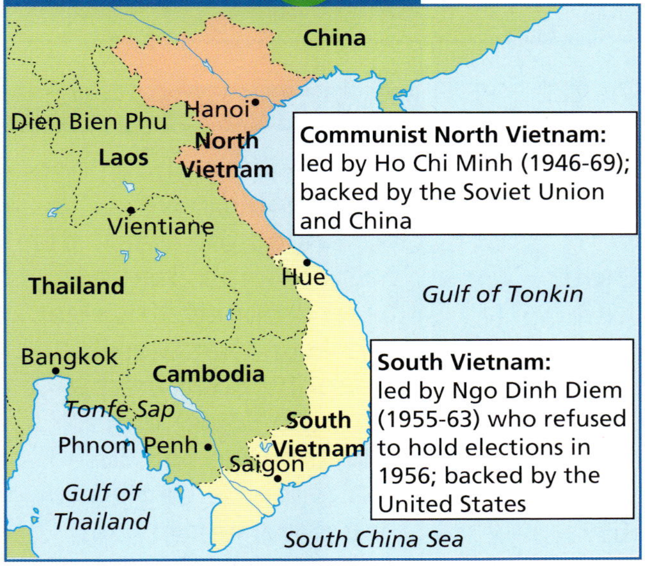
China
Hanoi
Dien Bien Phu
North Vietnam
Laos
Communist North Vietnam: led by Ho Chi Minh (1946-69); backed by the Soviet Union and China
Vientiane
Thailand
Hue
Gulf of Tonkin
Bangkok
Cambodia
Tonle Sap
South Vietnam: led by Ngo Dinh Diem (1955-63) who refused to hold elections in 1956; backed by the United States
South Vietnam
Phnom Penh
Saigon
Gulf of Thailand
South China Sea

▲ ***Map of Vietnam.***

RELIGION

In 1980 the Russians in Afghanistan suddenly found themselves in a very similar position to the Americans in Vietnam.

The Afghan government was anti-Muslim and supported the Soviet Union.

This had caused a lot of opposition in a Muslim country. In December 1979 Soviet troops went into Afghanistan to support the government there. They were afraid a successful Muslim revolution in Afghanistan might inspire Muslims in the Soviet Union to rebel as well.

By February 1980 there were 80,000 Soviet troops in Afghanistan. They found themselves fighting a very similar, guerrilla-style war to the one the Americans fought in Vietnam. The *mujaheddin*, as the Muslim fighters were called, wanted to free their country from foreign control and set up a government which would enforce Islamic laws.

By 1987 the Soviet leader, Mikhail Gorbachev, was looking for a way out of Afghanistan. By February 1989 all Soviet troops had pulled out – but not before 20,000 Russians had died.

SOURCE C

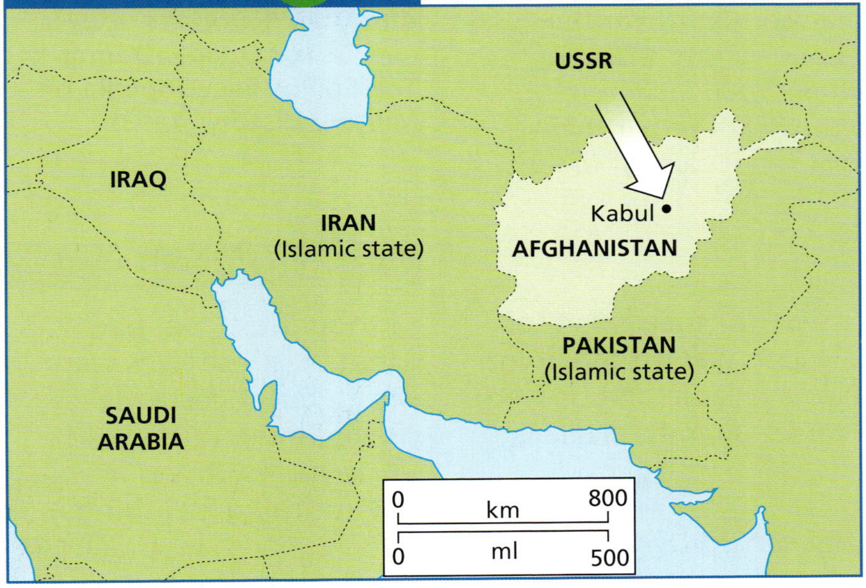
USSR
IRAQ
IRAN
(Islamic state)
Kabul
AFGHANISTAN
PAKISTAN
(Islamic state)
SAUDI ARABIA
0 km 800
0 ml 500

◄ ***Map of Afghanistan, showing Soviet invasion of 1979.***

Q *Think about it ...*

1. Explain how nationalism played a part in the wars in Vietnam and Afghanistan.
2. In what ways were these two wars different? (Think about the role of religion and Communism.)
3. Look at **Source C**. How does the map help to explain:

   a. Why the Soviet Union was worried about what happened in Afghanistan?

   b. Why were the *mujaheddin* in a good position to get military support from friendly countries?
4. Why do you think people who were fighting a war for nationalist and/or religious reasons often won against much more powerful opponents?

9 HOW DID THE COLD WAR START?

CHECK OUT THE LINK
How do wars start?: what were the long- and short-term causes of the twentieth century's conflicts?

WAS TRUMAN RIGHT TO USE THE ATOMIC BOMB?
The decision by the American president, Harry Truman, to use the atomic bomb on the cities of Hiroshima and Nagasaki in August 1945 has caused a great deal of debate among historians. The debate is a good example of how the same event can produce a variety of well-argued points of view.

In order to understand the range of views which historians have, it is important to know about the circumstances of the time. Germany had already surrendered in May of 1945 but no one knew how long the Japanese would go on fighting for. Previous experience of how the Japanese fought was not encouraging for the Americans. In the battle for Iwo Jima – a tiny island of mostly volcanic rock – 22,000 out of 23,000 Japanese defenders had chosen to fight to the death rather than surrender. How would they fight when it came it to defending Japan itself?

SOURCE A

No one knows how long Japan could have continued the war if the atomic bombs had not been dropped. It is clear, however, that these weapons, combined with the Soviet entry into the war, convinced the Japanese emperor and government that further resistance was hopeless.

▲ *From an account by two American historians, Ernest and Trevor Dupuy. Quoted in* **The Collins Encyclopedia of Military History** *(1993).*

SOURCE B

Atomic bombs did not win the war, for they came too late to decide who would win. Japan was on the point of surrender by the time the two available bombs were used…The war was won with tanks, aircraft, artillery, and submarines.

▲ *Quoted in* **Why the Allies Won,** *by Richard Overy (1995).*

SOURCE C

I still regret how the bombing was done. I realise that a threat was not enough. It had to be dropped somewhere. But there were other places they could have dropped it without such a terrible loss of life. Of course, some people thought of it as a warning to the Soviet Union: We're not going to be allies any longer, so don't get any ideas. We're stronger than you.

▲ *The view of an American scientist who helped to develop the bomb. Quoted in* **The Good War** *by Studs Terkel (1986).*

SOURCE D

I thought: 'I feel bad that all those lives were lost', but it certainly saved mine … It saved many lives. It was a beautiful, great thing.

▲ *The view of an American infantryman, Sheldon Johnson. He would have taken part in the American invasion of Japan if Japan had not surrendered on 14 August 1945. Quoted in* **Growing Up in the People's Century** *by John D Clare (1996).*

HOW DID THE COLD WAR START?

SOURCE E

By 1945 Japan had no fuel. This is what really defeated Japan. With or without the atomic bomb … Japan was finished, because her ships, aircraft, tanks and vehicles could not move.

▲ Quoted in **Truth: The First Casualty** by Philip Knightley (1975).

For this reason, in May 1945 Truman had asked the Russians to get involved in the war against Japan as well and the Soviet Union agreed to declare war on Japan in August. In the three months between May and August relations between the Soviet Union and Britain and the USA began to get a little frosty as the early stages of the Cold War started to set in. Now, in August, the Americans weren't so sure it was a good idea to have Russian troops on Japanese soil.

SOURCE F

▲ Japanese soldiers lie among the ruins of Tarawa after a battle with US marines.

WAS THERE AN ALTERNATIVE?

Some people have argued that Truman could have warned the Japanese about the attack so that the cities could have been evacuated. Perhaps a bomb could have been used on an area where there were no people. Either way, the Japanese would have seen the terrible power of the bomb without the loss of civilian lives. Would a 'demonstration' have had any affect on the Japanese government? The death of 80,000 civilians on March 9 1945 in the Tokyo fire-bombing had little effect on the government's will to fight on. It's also worth pointing out that the Americans only had two nuclear bombs. If they used them as a demonstration and they had no effect, it would be months before they could build others. In the meantime, how many more American lives would be lost?

SOURCE G

▲ A group of kamikaze or suicide pilots pose for a last picture before flying their planes, packed with explosives, against American ships. By the time the Second World War ended, 5,000 pilots had volunteered for this certain death, sinking 36 ships and damaging nearly 400 more. Many more Japanese were ready to do the same.

Q *Think about it …*

'The use of the atomic bombs was unnecessary. Japan was already beaten.'
Using the sources and the text, explain in a short essay whether you agree or disagree with this view. Remember to finish with a conclusion which makes clear what your view is. Perhaps you could say what the most important reason which supports your view is, and why.

10 WHY WAS THERE A COLD WAR AFTER THE SECOND WORLD WAR?

CHECK OUT THE LINK
Why did the Cold War not lead to a 'hot' war?

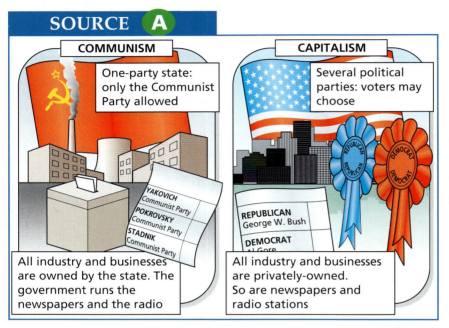

◀ *The differences between Communism and Capitalism.*

The origins of the Cold War between the USA and the Soviet Union go back to 1917 when the Communists in Russia carried out a successful revolution. The USA and the rest of Europe believed in capitalism and democracy. From then on, Communism was feared and hated in the West, especially in the USA (see **Source A**).

Churchill and Truman suspected that Stalin, the leader of the Soviet Union, was trying to spread Soviet Communism around the world. Stalin suspected that Churchill and Truman were looking for ways to destroy Communism. Now that the Americans had this terrible new weapon – the atomic bomb – they had the power to do it. Relations between the old allies became frosty: the Cold War had started.

EUROPE AFTER 1945

This tension between the former allies first showed itself in Europe. Stalin was convinced that the western powers – Britain, France and the USA – were plotting to invade the Soviet Union and start another war. He decided that Russia needed to be protected from invasion by creating a ring of friendly, Communist countries around it. These countries were already under Soviet control because the Red Army had occupied them while defeating the Germans.

One by one, these countries became Communist (see **Source B**). By the end of 1948 Poland, Czechoslovakia, Hungary, Romania, Bulgaria, East Germany and Albania all had Communist governments. Yugoslavia was also Communist but it was not under Soviet control. The other countries of Europe had democratic governments, supported by the USA.

In 1946, Churchill used the phrase 'the iron curtain' to describe the division between the communist half of Europe in the east and the democratic half in the west. The iron part of the 'curtain' was the barbed wire fence which now kept each side apart.

DIVIDED GERMANY

Germany was a special problem for the Soviet Union and the West. The western part of Germany was controlled by Britain, France and the USA, while the eastern part was controlled by the Russians. Berlin, the capital of Germany, was divided in exactly the same way but it was deep inside the Soviet zone (**Source C**).

WHY WAS THERE A COLD WAR AFTER THE SECOND WORLD WAR?

SOURCE B

▲ Map of Europe in 1949, after the Second World War.

 Think about it …

1. Copy the map (**Source B**) onto a piece of paper.

a. Think of a form of shading or colour to use to show the Communist countries of Europe under Russian control by the end of 1948. Do *not* include Yugoslavia.

b. Think of another shade or colour for Yugoslavia as a Communist country but not under Russian control.

c. Use another colour or shade to show the non-Communist or democratic states of Europe.

d. Use a pencil or colour to draw a thick line from Trieste, between Yugoslavia and Italy, to Lubeck (between East and West Germany) so that East Germany, Czechoslovakia, Yugoslavia and Hungary are all to the east of the line. This represents the Iron Curtain.

e. Finally, fill in the boxes in the key to show the correct colour or shade which you have used.

2. Looking at the map of Europe in 1949, why might Stalin be

a. pleased with what he saw

b. displeased with what he saw?

In 1948 Stalin decided that he wanted to control all of Berlin and not just its eastern half. Since Berlin was deep inside the Soviet zone of Germany it was an easy matter to shut off all road and rail routes into West Berlin. In this way, the western powers would be forced to give up West Berlin and the Russians would occupy it. Instead, the Americans, British and French brought food and fuel supplies to the city by air ('the Berlin Airlift') for 13 months.

Eventually, Stalin realised he couldn't starve West Berlin and gave up. He reopened the rail and road routes to the city in 1949. Stalin was aware that the Soviet Union was a long way behind the USA in nuclear technology (Russia didn't have its own nuclear bomb until August 1949) and so couldn't risk a war.

THE COLD WAR GOES GLOBAL

There was some good news for Stalin at the end of the decade. In October 1949, China's Communists finally took control of the country after two decades of war. Now the country with the biggest population in the world was also Communist. However, a plan to spread Communism elsewhere in South East Asia didn't go according to plan. The invasion of South Korea by Communist North Korea led to the Korean War (1950–53) but the invaders were defeated, mainly because the USA sent 400,000 troops to defend South Korea.

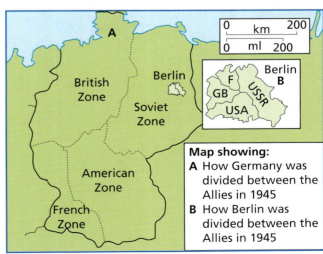

▲ Map of Germany and Berlin.

11 WHY DID THE COLD WAR NOT LEAD TO A 'HOT' WAR?

CHECK OUT THE LINK
Do you think the Cuban Missile Crisis might have ended differently if Stalin, or a leader like him, had still been in control of the Soviet Union?

During the 1950s, relations between the USA and the Soviet Union got better, got worse, and then got better again. Relations improved because Stalin died in 1953 and the man who took over as leader of the Soviet Union, Nikita Khrushchev, wanted better relations with the West.

THE HUNGARIAN RISING

However, a crisis in 1956 caused a set-back in the improved relations. In that year, the Hungarians tried to break away from Russian control. In November 1956 the Soviet leader, Nikita Khruschev, sent troops into Hungary and 20,000 Hungarians were killed in the fighting which followed. The Russians made sure that the new government in Hungary obeyed the Soviet leaders. The leader of the anti-Soviet Hungarians, Imre Nagy, was hanged by the Russians.

SOURCE B

I had the idea of installing missiles with nuclear warheads. We had no desire to start a war. We sent the Americans a note that we agreed to remove our missiles on the condition that there would be no invasion of Cuba by the forces of the USA or anyone else. Finally, Kennedy gave in and agreed to make a statement promising to do this. It was a great victory for us.

▲ *From Khrushchev's memoirs*, Khrushchev Remembers (1971).

In 1961 the Communist government in East Germany built a wall dividing West and East Berlin so that no East Berliners could escape into West Berlin. The wall literally divided families in two. Relatives living in East Berlin couldn't vist their families in the western part of the city. Perhaps as many as 200 East Berliners have lost their lives trying to cross the wall.

THE BAY OF PIGS INCIDENT

Relations became even more icy in 1962. In this year the world came the closest ever to a Third World War. In 1959 Fidel Castro led a successful revolution against the government of Cuba. The old Cuban government cared little for the poor and looked after the interests of Cuban and American businesses. The Americans immediately acted against Castro. They accused him of being a Communist and working for the Russians. The Americans were worried because Cuba is only 150km (90 miles) from the American coast.

The US Central Intelligence Agency (CIA) came up with a plan to overthrow Castro using a force of 1,500 anti-Castro Cubans which would invade Cuba. The invasion force landed at the Bay of Pigs in April 1961. It was a total flop. Castro, fearing another invasion, asked the Russians to set up nuclear missiles in Cuba.

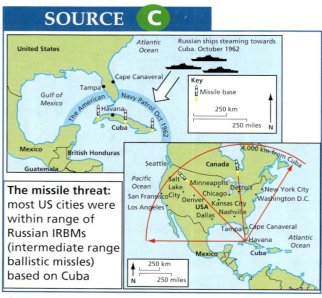

SOURCE C

The missile threat: most US cities were within range of Russian IRBMs (intermediate range ballistic missiles) based on Cuba

▲ *Map of Cuba, 1962.*

WHY DID THE COLD WAR NOT LEAD TO A 'HOT WAR'?

SOURCE D

When one side is clearly wrong, it will eventually give way. That is what happened here. They had no business putting those missiles in and lying to me about it. They were in the wrong and they knew it. So, when we stood firm, they had to back down.

▲ Kennedy's view of the crisis in a private conversation with Arthur Schlesinger; quoted in Schlesinger's *A Thousand Days* (1965).

THE CUBAN MISSILE CRISIS, 1962

In October 1962, the USA discovered that there were 42 Soviet nuclear missiles on Cuba. Kennedy considered his options. He could order an air strike against the missile sites in Cuba. Indeed, he could order full invasion of Cuba. Either of these would probably lead to war with Russia. The third option was to use the navy to seal off the island to stop more missiles arriving and to negotiate with Khrushchev. Kennedy chose the third option.

Kennedy demanded that Khrushchev remove the missiles from Cuba and take them back to Russia. In the meantime, he ordered the US Navy to patrol around Cuba and stop and search any Russian ships approaching the island. Khrushchev agreed to remove the missiles – but only if the USA removed its missiles from Turkey and if Kennedy promised that the USA would never invade Cuba.

 Think about it ...

1. Look at the map of Cuba (**Source C**). How does it explain why the Americans were so worried about Russian missiles on the island?

2. **a.** In what ways do **Sources B** and **D** give different views of the missile crisis?

   b. Which one do you think is closer to the truth? Explain your answer.

3. Copy the diagram in **Source E**. Three of the boxes can be described as 'causes' of the Cold War and the rest as 'effects' of the Cold War. Use one form of shading for the causes boxes and another for the effects. Now write a brief essay explaining how the cold war started in 1945 and what its main events were up to the Cuban Missile Crisis.

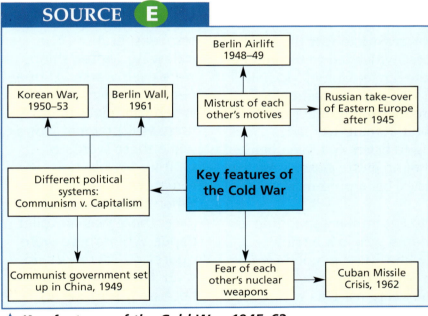

▲ Key features of the Cold War, 1945–62.

Kennedy did not want to look as though he was being bullied by the Russians. *Officially*, he agreed to promise never to invade Cuba but said nothing about the missiles in Turkey. *Privately*, Kennedy did offer to withdraw some US missiles from bases in Europe, including Turkey. Khrushchev was by now as worried as Kennedy that both sides were heading for a war neither wanted. He decided to accept Kennedy's offer and agreed to take the missiles away from Cuba. The crisis was over. War was avoided because both men had the good sense to realise that a nuclear war would mean the destruction of both their countries and that there could be no winner.

12 HOW DID THE COLD WAR END?

SOURCE A

NEW WORDS

MEDIUM RANGE MISSILES: these weapons were used for targets between 800km and 2400km away.

◀ *The Berlin Wall comes down, November 1989. Berliners, from both sides of Berlin, celebrate the end of Communism in Germany and its hated symbol – the Berlin Wall.*

The most important reason the Cold War lasted for 45 years from 1945 to 1990 was fear: the fear which came from the knowledge that the each side had the power to destroy the other. As a result, both sides built up huge stocks of nuclear weapons to maintain this threat. If one side got the advantage over the other, then it had to make up the difference and go one better. The Cold War could only end when each side no longer had any reason to fear the other.

The man who started the process which led to the end of the Cold War was the leader of the Soviet Union, Mikhail Gorbachev. He became leader in 1985 and immediately made it clear that he wanted to reduce the number of nuclear weapons which Russia had. Ronald Reagan, President of the USA, was willing to listen. In December 1987, both men agreed to get rid of an entire class of nuclear weapons: **medium-range missiles**. This represented 3,800 nuclear warheads.

Gorbachev had no choice but to cut military spending as far as possible. The Russian economy was in a terrible condition. Living standards were low. Russian goods were of very poor quality because the Soviet Union was spending about 20 per cent of its wealth on weapons. This was money it couldn't afford. That money needed to be spent on making the lives of ordinary Russians better. Perhaps some of it could be spent on making better television sets – between 1982 and 1987 18,000 Russian-made TVs exploded, killing 1,000 people.

Gorbachev encouraged Russians to criticise the Communist system so that improvements could be made. He hoped that improving people's lives and changing the system would make Communism work better. Unfortunately for Gorbachev, he started a process which he later found he could not stop. People weren't happy with changing the Communist system to make it work better – they wanted to get rid of it altogether.

SOURCE B

The winter before August 1991, food shortages brought the Russians to the point of total desperation. The following winter, things were even worse. At one point there was no milk. When there was milk, there was no meat. For a while there were no sanitary towels, no tomatoes, no shoes. When there was fruit juice, there was no toilet paper. When there were cigarettes, there was no soap. Factories closed because there was no heat. Communism turned out to be the worst economic disaster in the history of the world … Until recently, everything was always sold at a loss. A loaf of bread used to cost 20 kopeks to buy but 60 kopeks to bake.

▲ *From* The End of the American Century *by Jeffrey Robinson (1997).*

HOW DID THE COLD WAR END?

SOURCE D

▲ The end of the Cold War did not bring peace. It led a to a vicious civil war in what used to be Yugoslavia as Serbs, Croats and Muslims fought each other.

SOURCE C

Eduard Shevarnadze [the Soviet foreign minster under Gorbachev] reckoned that as much as 50% of the Soviet Union's national income was spent on defence, arms, and the armed forces, depriving the Soviet people of a better life. In the United States spending on national defence ran at over 10% of national income in the 1950s and 6% in the 1980s.

▲ From The Cold War by Jeremy Isaacs and Taylor Downing (1998).

THE COLLAPSE OF COMMUNISM

Gorbachev's decision to allow more freedom in Russia encouraged the peoples of eastern Europe to do the same. They too wanted an end to Communism and they wanted the freedom to rule themselves, without having to obey Russia. Gorbachev realised that he couldn't control eastern Europe and carry out the changes he wanted inside Russia. He allowed the Communist states of eastern Europe to do as they pleased. They weren't slow to seize their chance.

In November 1989 the East German government declared that the Berlin Wall would be opened so that East and West Germans could mix freely. People stood on it and hacked chunks out of it (see **Source A**). One by one the former Communist states of eastern Europe abandoned Communism and began to elect democratic governments. Then it was Russia's turn. In August 1991, Communist army leaders tried to overthrow Gorbachev and put a stop to the changes he had introduced. Gorbachev was arrested but the plot failed when units of the army fought off the Communist troops. Gorbachev was free but the people didn't want him or his 'improved' Communist system. By the end of 1991 Gorbachev was out of power, Soviet Communism was finished, and so was the Soviet Union. Russia was no longer a superpower. The USA had 'won' the Cold War.

 Think about it ...

1. Why, according to the text, did Gorbachev have to cut the money Russia spent on weapons?

2. How do **Sources B** and **C** support your answer to question 1?

3. 'The Cold War ended because Russia couldn't afford to keep spending on weapons.' How far do you agree with this interpretation? You could use the following points to help you:

■ the problems military spending caused Russia

■ how Gorbachev's solution went wrong

■ consider whether the Communist system would have continued for much longer anyway.

13 LOCAL HISTORY AND THE GREAT WAR

It isn't difficult to find out how the last century's conflicts affected your local area. There's a great deal of evidence to find if you know where to look or whom to ask. Wherever you live in Britain you should be able to learn, for example, about the First and Second World Wars from a number of sources:

- local war memorials;
- interviews with older relatives;
- photographs;
- local newspapers of the time.

NEW WORDS
ACTIVE SERVICE: combat in the front line.

PUTTING THE PIECES TOGETHER
Getting information about a local person who died during either the First or Second World War is like putting together various pieces of a jigsaw puzzle. This is how one school in Buckinghamshire set about finding out what it could about one of the men who died in the First World War.

In 1990 the history department of my school in Chesham decided that it would like to lay a wreath in honour of one of the men from the town who was killed in the Great War. So we went to the offices of our local newspaper and asked to look through the back issues of the paper from the 1914–18 period. We soon had a list of names of men and their regiments. We wrote to the Commonwealth War Graves Commission and asked them to tell us where these men were buried. Unfortunately, they couldn't provide us with any precise details about which cemeteries these men were buried in without their service numbers.

So we tried a different approach. The department wrote to the letters page of the local paper and in the letter we said that we were visiting the battlefields of the First World War. We said that we would like to lay a wreath in honour of any local men on behalf of their relatives. We soon received a letter from an 85-year-old woman, Mrs May Brandon, and we went to visit her in Chesham.

SOURCE A

▲ George Payne is sitting in the middle row on the right with glasses. The picture seems to have been taken in 1917 when he was still in the Army Service Corps.

GEORGE'S STORY
Mrs May Brandon told us about her brother, George Payne. George worked in the local bakery – which is still owned by the same family – and in 1915 he decided to volunteer for the army. He was 20 at the time. George had poor eyesight and wore glasses so the army decided he wasn't fit for **active service**. They gave him a safe job as a baker in the Army Service Corps instead. His mother was relieved but George was probably disappointed.

However, in 1918 the army was getting short of men for active service. The fact that George wore glasses didn't seem to matter any more.

LOCAL HISTORY AND THE GREAT WAR

He was sent to a front-line regiment but May couldn't remember which one or the day he was killed. The cemetery register at Tyne Cot, at Ypres in Belgium, told us that he had been transferred to the Inniskilling Fusiliers and that he was killed on 15 October – less than a month before the war ended. It also told us his parents' names and their address in Chesham. On 9 November – two days before the war ended – George's parents received the dreaded telegram telling them that their son had been killed in action.

THE DAY MAY'S FATHER CRIED

May was 13 at the time. She told us how she still remembered the day the telegram arrived and what a terrible day it was. Her mother had just taught her to use a sewing machine. She came into the kitchen of their small terraced house in Chesham to find her father sobbing, his head resting on his arms on the kitchen table. It was, May said, the first and the only time she saw her father cry. Her mother, broken-hearted, died two years later. She was never able to get over the loss of her son.

Perhaps even more distressing for May's family was the fact that they were never able to visit George's grave because he had no grave. His body was never found. Instead, his name was chiselled into the stone memorial which surrounds Tyne Cot cemetery. The 42 pupils and staff made their way to the memorial wall and we laid our wreath there. May's story is a very sad one but no different to the 700,000 stories of families up and down the length of the British Isles, who also lost loved ones in those painful years. The local paper decided to run a full page feature on George's story and on our trip to the battlefields of Belgium and northern France. We were glad that Mrs Brandon was able to tell her story because it made the visit that much more personal and meaningful for all of us and because Mrs Brandon herself died six months later.

SOURCE A

▲ Pupils laying a wreath beside the name of George Payne carved on the stone memorial to the 35,000 British soldiers who were killed in the Ypres area but whose bodies were never found.

 Think about it ...

Carrying out your own research

It will be very difficult to find people today who have first-hand memories of the First World War and how it affected them. But everything we did for our First World War research applies to the Second World War. Your local war memorial will have names of those who died and your local newspaper will probably have details of these men's stories. If your own family has been in your area for 60 years or more then you will be able to talk to them directly about their experiences there or wherever they were at the time.

To prepare for your investigation, think about the type of questions you could ask. Your questions will need to be different, depending on whether you are interviewing someone who was on active service or someone who spent the war years on the 'home front'.

14 WHY WERE SO MANY PEOPLE AFFECTED?

In Chapter 2 we looked how the conflicts of the twentieth century were different from other conflicts, especially after 1945. The Second World War, for example, has been described by historians as the first 'total' war. This is because the role of civilians was as important as those of the men in the front line, and they were greatly involved in the dangers. The Cold War affected the entire population of the planet in a way which the Second World War never did. If the Cold War had turned into a 'hot' Third World War, everyone would have been affected by the terrible consequences of a 'nuclear winter'. Even those who survived would have been at risk from the clouds of radiation blown across the world, contaminating food and animals as well as people.

ACCIDENTS WILL HAPPEN …

There was (and still is) the risk of a nuclear accident. The USA equipped its hydrogen bombs with six failsafe devices. Each device was enough to prevent an accidental explosion. In 1961 one of several nuclear accidents took place when a US bomber broke up in mid-air over the USA. The plane was carrying two 24 megaton nuclear bombs which fell to earth. Neither bomb exploded. One was never found – it sank into waterlogged farmland. The American military was feeling rather pleased with the success of their failsafe devices until they recovered the other bomb. Five of its six failsafe devices had *failed* to work. North Carolina was saved from an explosion 16,000 times more destructive than the Hiroshima bomb by just one failsafe device.

SOURCE A

▲ This is how American school-children were told to react if a nuclear attack threatened. Sit in the corridor and cover your heads. The teachers, it would seem, were safer standing up.

SOURCE B

▲ This was the first ever photograph of an American hydrogen bomb. It was recovered undamaged from the Mediterranean Sea in 1966 off the coast of Spain, after a US bomber blew up in mid-air during a refuelling accident.

WHY WERE SO MANY PEOPLE AFFECTED?

SOURCE C

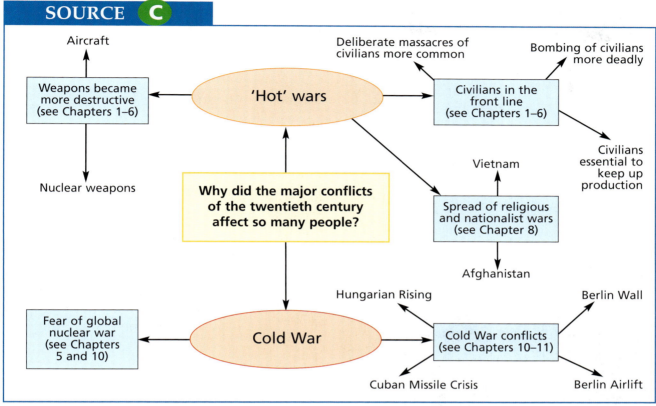

▲ Why did the conflicts of the twentieth century affect so many people?

 Think about it ...

Your task is to write an essay in answer to the question 'Why did the conflicts of the twentieth century affect so many people?' The diagram (**Source C**) will help you with this. Each of the five blue boxes provides an outline for a paragraph. You could start your essay as follows:

- Introduction: Explain how the twentieth century has seen different types of conflict – 'hot' wars and a Cold War which lasted until about 1990.

  Paragraph 1: Using Chapters 1–6 for information, explain how weapons have become much more destructive and how this has affected civilians.

- Paragraph 2: Explain how wars have been caused for many different reasons, involving different beliefs and large numbers of people.

- Paragraph 3: Show how the invention of nuclear weapons created a threat to the whole planet. Use Hiroshima as an example of the terrible power of these weapons and the Cuban Missile Crisis as an example of the dangers.

- Paragraph 4: Explain how many people's lives continued to be affected by several little 'hot wars' after 1945.

- Conclusion: Sum up by saying what you think has been the most important reason why so many people were affected by wars in the twentieth century.

Index

Afghanistan War	17
Armenian genocide	7
Bay of Pigs (1961)	22
Berlin	20–21, 22
Bosnia	7, 14
Capitalism	20
Central Intelligence Agency (CIA)	22
Chamberlain, Neville	15
Churchill, Winston	20
Civilians and war	6–7
Communism	20
Conscription	12
Cuban Missiles Crisis (1962)	22–23
First World War	6, 8, 12, 14
First World War causes	14
France	16
Genocide	7
Germany	14–15
Gorbachev, Mikhail	17, 24–25
Gulf War (1991)	11
Hiroshima	2–3, 4, 11, 18–19
Hungarian Rising (1956)	22
Islam	17
Kennedy, John F	22–23
Khrushchev, Nikita	22–23
Korean War (1950–53)	21
Kosovo (1999)	11
Munich Conference	15
Nazi–Soviet Pact	15
Pakistan	7
Patriotism and War	12
Reagan, Ronald	24
Religion	7, 17
Second World War	6, 8–9, 12, 14, 28
Second World War causes	14–15
Serbia	14
Soviet Union (Russia)	3, 4, 11, 17, 20–21
Stalin, Joseph	20–21
Technology and war	10–11
Treaty of Versailles	14
Truman, Harry S.	18–19
United States	3, 11, 16, 17
Vietnam Wars	12, 16
Women role in war	8–9